6/16 $25

 W9-BWB-578

DATE DUE

SUPER CUTE!

Baby
Koalas

by Megan Borgert-Spaniol

BELLWETHER MEDIA • MINNEAPOLIS, MN

Note to Librarians, Teachers, and Parents:

Blastoff! Readers are carefully developed by literacy experts and combine standards-based content with developmentally appropriate text.

Level 1 provides the most support through repetition of high-frequency words, light text, predictable sentence patterns, and strong visual support.

Level 2 offers early readers a bit more challenge through varied simple sentences, increased text load, and less repetition of high-frequency words.

Level 3 advances early-fluent readers toward fluency through increased text and concept load, less reliance on visuals, longer sentences, and more literary language.

Level 4 builds reading stamina by providing more text per page, increased use of punctuation, greater variation in sentence patterns, and increasingly challenging vocabulary.

Level 5 encourages children to move from "learning to read" to "reading to learn" by providing even more text, varied writing styles, and less familiar topics.

Whichever book is right for your reader, Blastoff! Readers are the perfect books to build confidence and encourage a love of reading that will last a lifetime!

This edition first published in 2016 by Bellwether Media, Inc.

No part of this publication may be reproduced in whole or in part without written permission of the publisher. For information regarding permission, write to Bellwether Media, Inc., Attention: Permissions Department, 5357 Penn Avenue South, Minneapolis, MN 55419.

Library of Congress Cataloging-in-Publication Data

Borgert-Spaniol, Megan, 1989- author.
  Baby Koalas / by Megan Borgert-Spaniol.
    pages cm. – (Blastoff! Readers. Super Cute!)
  Summary: "Developed by literacy experts for students in kindergarten through grade three, this book introduces baby koalas to young readers through leveled text and related photos"– Provided by publisher.
  Audience: Ages 5-8
  Audience: K to grade 3
  Includes bibliographical references and index.
  ISBN 978-1-62617-219-7 (hardcover: alk. paper)
  1. Koala–Infancy–Juvenile literature. I. Title. II. Series: Blastoff! Readers. 1, Super Cute!
  QL737.M384B67 2016
  599.2'5–dc23

                          2015009721

Printed in the United States of America, North Mankato, MN.

Table of Contents

Koala Joey!

A baby koala is called a joey. A **newborn** joey is the size of a jelly bean.

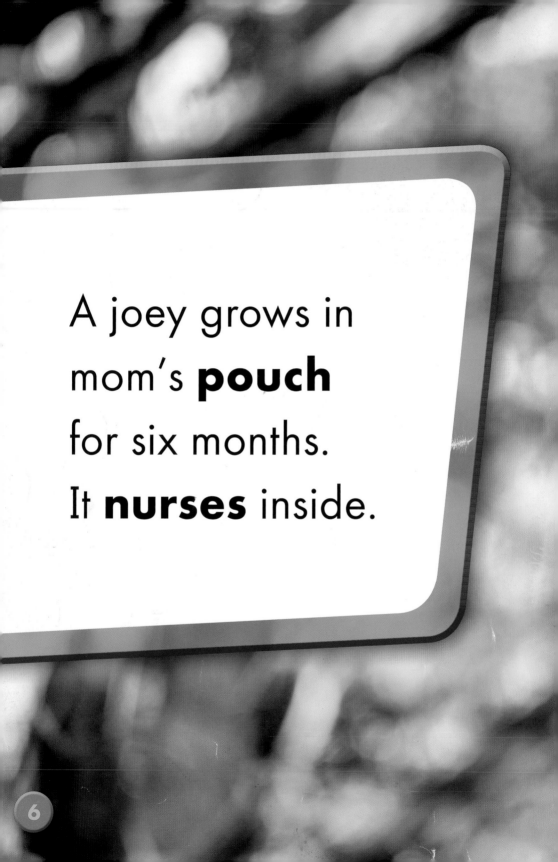

A joey grows in
mom's **pouch**
for six months.
It **nurses** inside.

Then the joey climbs out of the pouch. It returns to rest or hide.

Out of the Pouch

Soon the joey is too big for the pouch. It **clings** to mom's chest.

Sometimes
it rides on
mom's back.

The joey naps
with mom in the
trees. They are
safe there.

The joey grabs leaves with its mouth. Later it eats with its hands.

A New Home

The joey stays with mom for about a year. Then it finds a tree of its own.

This joey found a comfortable branch. Sleep well, joey!

Glossary

clings—holds on tightly

newborn—just recently born

nurses—drinks mom's milk

pouch—a pocket of skin on the belly of a female koala

To Learn More

AT THE LIBRARY
Kawa, Katie. *Baby Koalas*. New York, N.Y.:
Gareth Stevens Pub., 2012.

Marsh, Laura. *Koalas*. Washington, D.C.:
National Geographic, 2014.

Schuetz, Kari. *Koalas*. Minneapolis, Minn.:
Bellwether Media, 2012.

ON THE WEB
Learning more about koalas
is as easy as 1, 2, 3.

1. Go to www.factsurfer.com.

2. Enter "koalas" into the search box.

3. Click the "Surf" button and you will see a
   list of related web sites.

With factsurfer.com, finding more information
is just a click away.

Index

The images in this book are reproduced through the courtesy of: worldswildlifewonders, front cover, pp. 4-5, 18-19; Bruce & Jan Lichtenberger/ Glow Images, pp. 6-7; Boyloso, pp. 6-7 (bottom); Suzi Eszterhas/ Minden Pictures/ Corbis, pp. 8-9, 10-11; inlovepai, pp. 8-9 (bottom); KWL, pp. 10-11 (bottom); ZSSD/ Minden Pictures/ Corbis, pp. 12-13, 14-15; McPhoto/ Age Fotostock, pp. 16-17; Shay Yacobinski, pp. 16-17 (bottom); ChaiwatPhotos, pp. 18-19 (bottom); Picture Press/ Alamy, pp. 20-21.